Get in touch with us for more expository books, journals, & great freebies.

EMAIL: palinco2003@yahoo.com

www.bookspillar.blogspot.com

Number Tracing Mastery For Ages 2-4.

Number Tracing

Book For Ages 2-4.

I can see one apple.

1

1 One

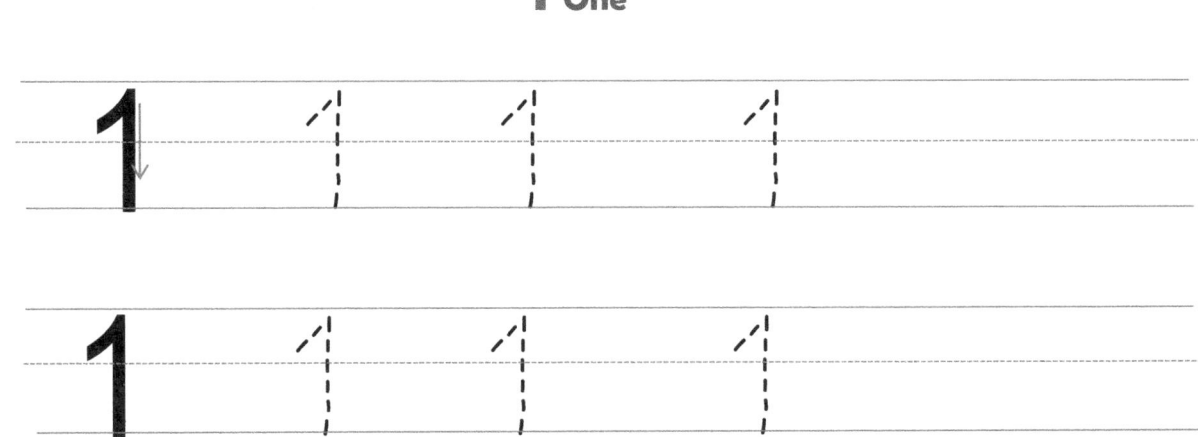

How many **birds** are there? Two birds.

2 Two

2

2

2

2

2

2

2

2

2

There are three butterflies here.

3 Three

3

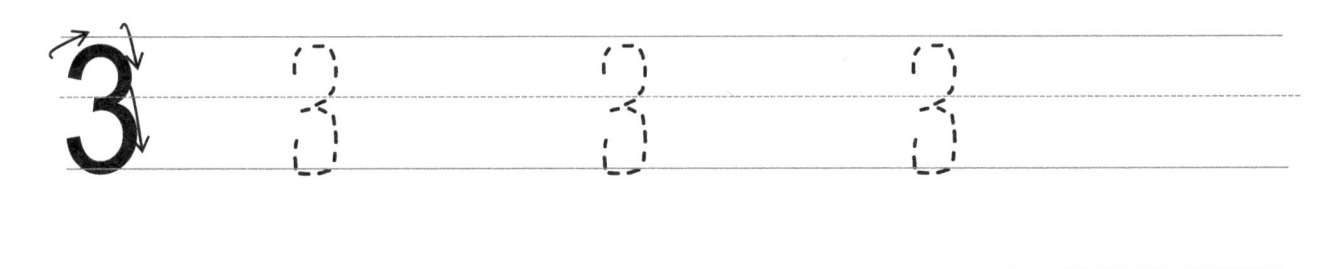

Four leaves in different shapes.

4

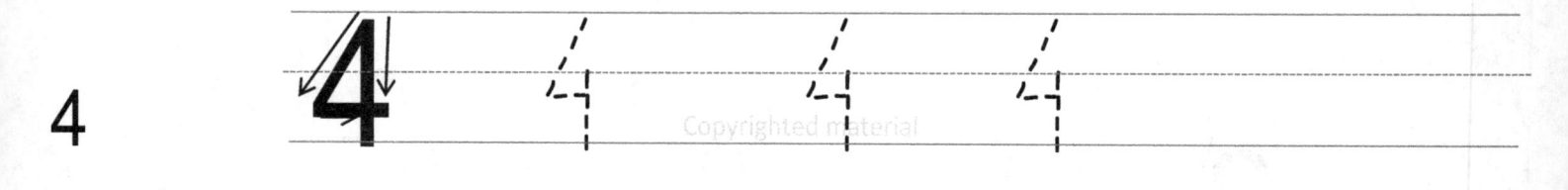

I can see five trucks.

Five.

5 Five

5

5   5   5   5

5   5   5   5

There are six **buses here.**

6 Six

Six.

6

6   6   6   6

6   6   6   6

I can count seven jeep vehicles above.

Seven

7

7 7 7 7

7 7 7 7

I can see eight **cars.**

Eight

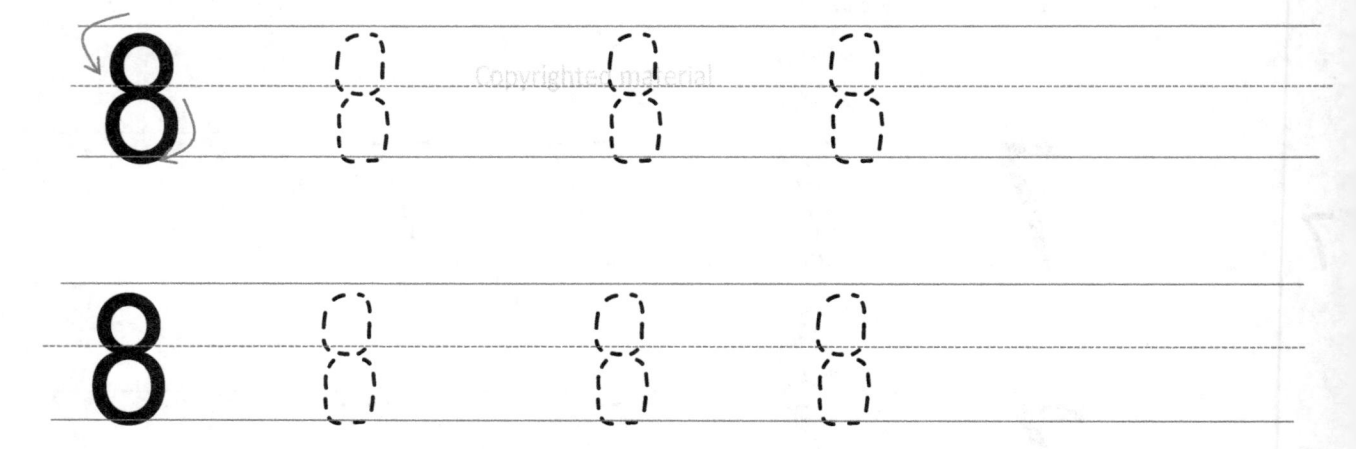

8

Nine juicy slices of water melon.

9 Nine

Nine

9

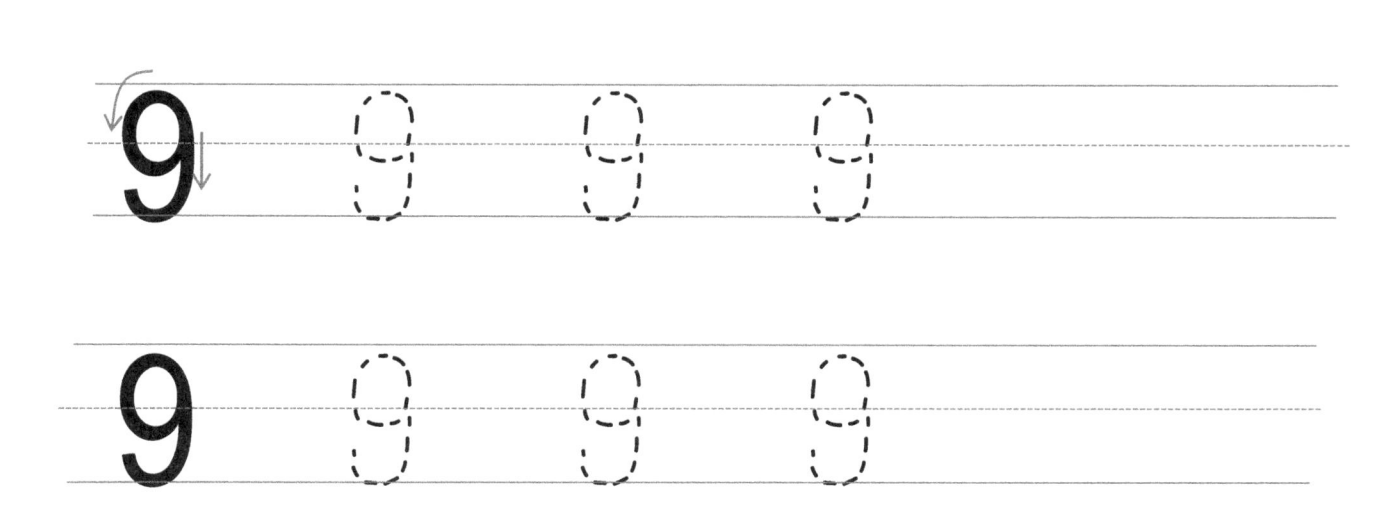

Count and circle each of the ten pineapples.

10 **Ten**

Ten

10

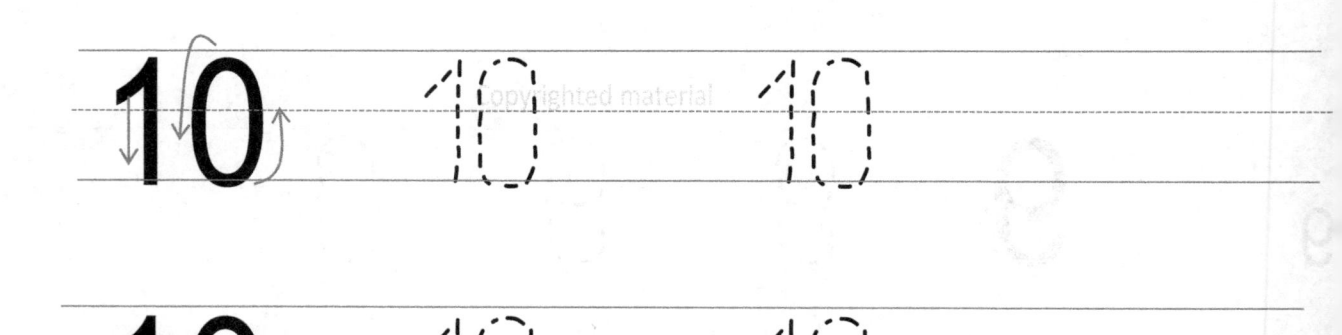

I can see eleven ducks. Can you count them?   **11 Eleven**

Eleven

11

11   11   11

11   11   11

I can count twelve pencils here.

12 Twelve

Twelve

12

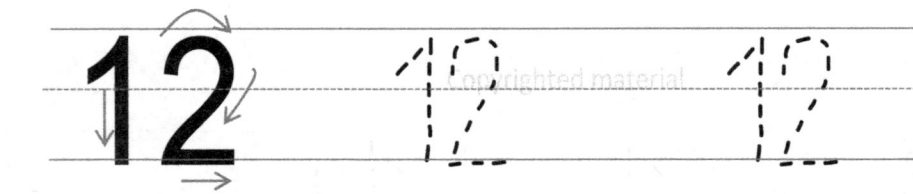

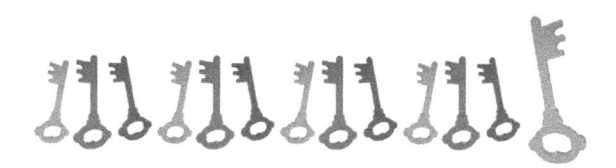

I can count thirteen keys. Circle the biggest key among them.

Thirteen

13 Thirteen

13

13   13   13

13   13   13

I see fourteen dolls here.

Fourteen

14 Fourteen

14

14 14 14

14 14 14

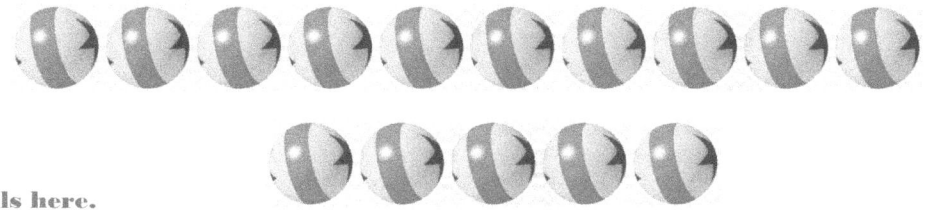

There are fifteen balls here.

Fifteen

15 **Fifteen**

15

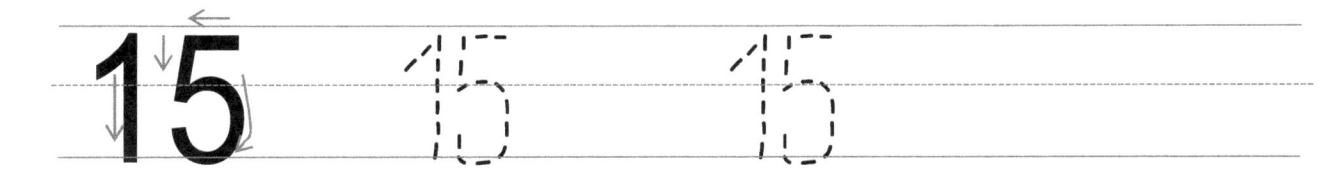

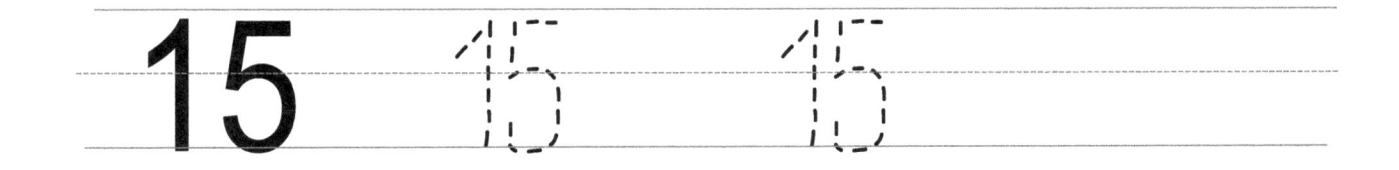

I can see sixteen wristwatches here.

16 Sixteen

16

16 16 16

16 16 16

Sixteen

I can see seventeen cutleries. Spot and circle the longest one among them.

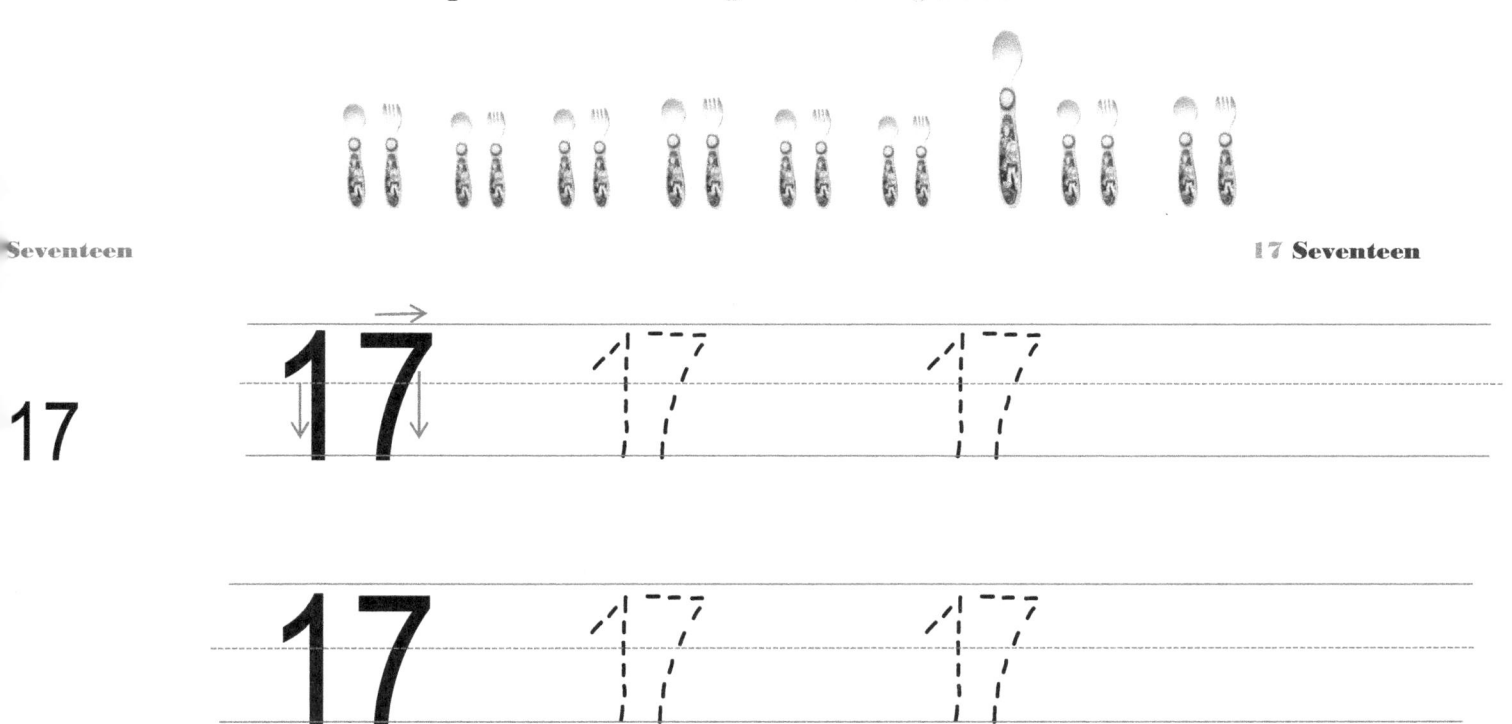

Seventeen

17 Seventeen

17

17 17 17

17 17 17

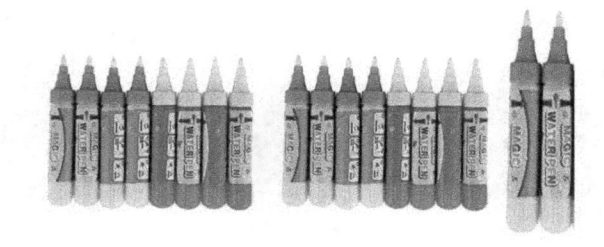

Eighteen pens are here. Which two are the longest?

18

18 18 18

18 18 18

I can count nineteen **fish here.**

19

19   19   19

19   19   19

I can see twenty brushes above.

Twenty 20 Twenty

20

20 20 20

20 20 20

Section Two:

Practice more tracing for numbers and their spellings.

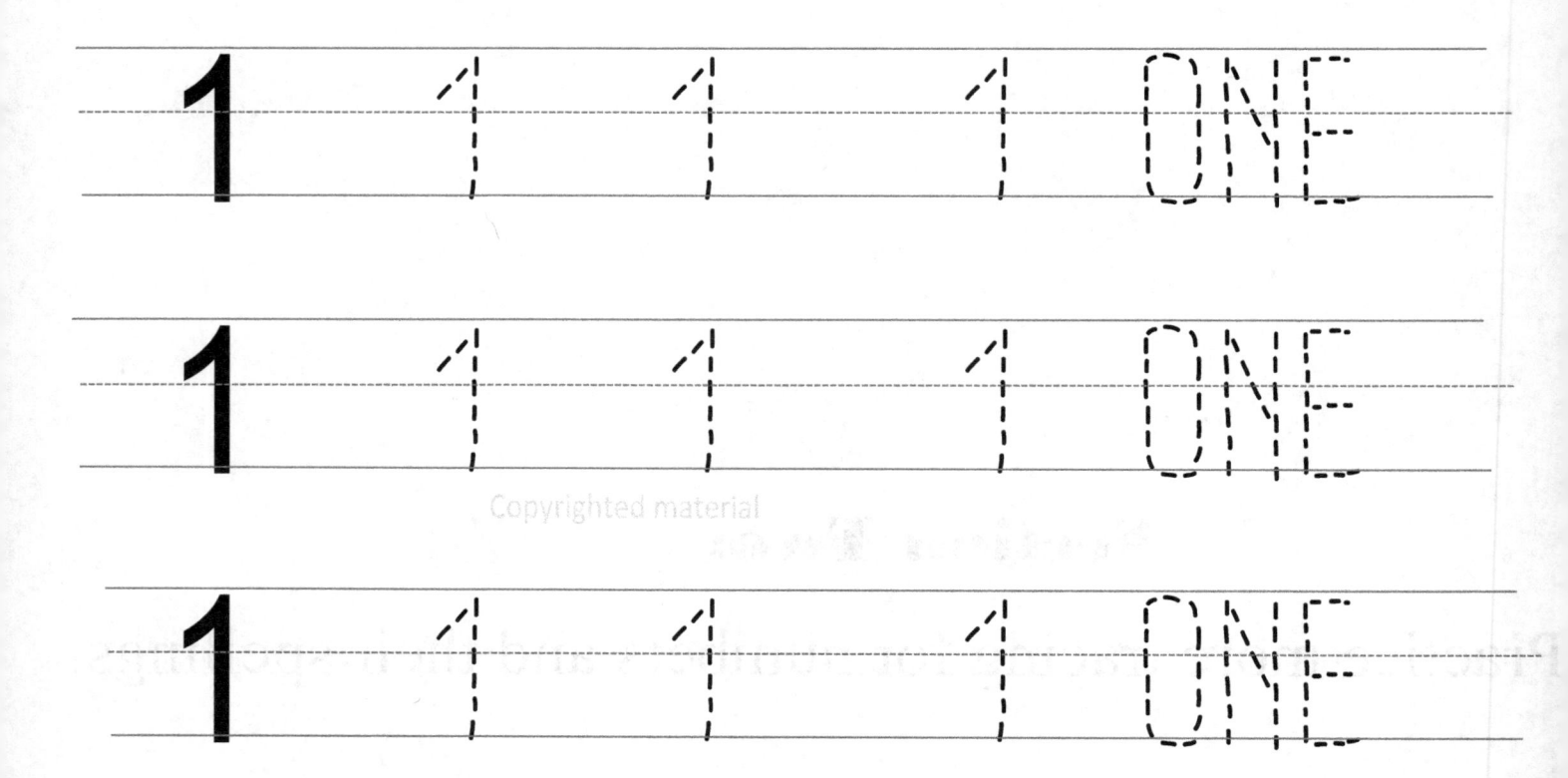

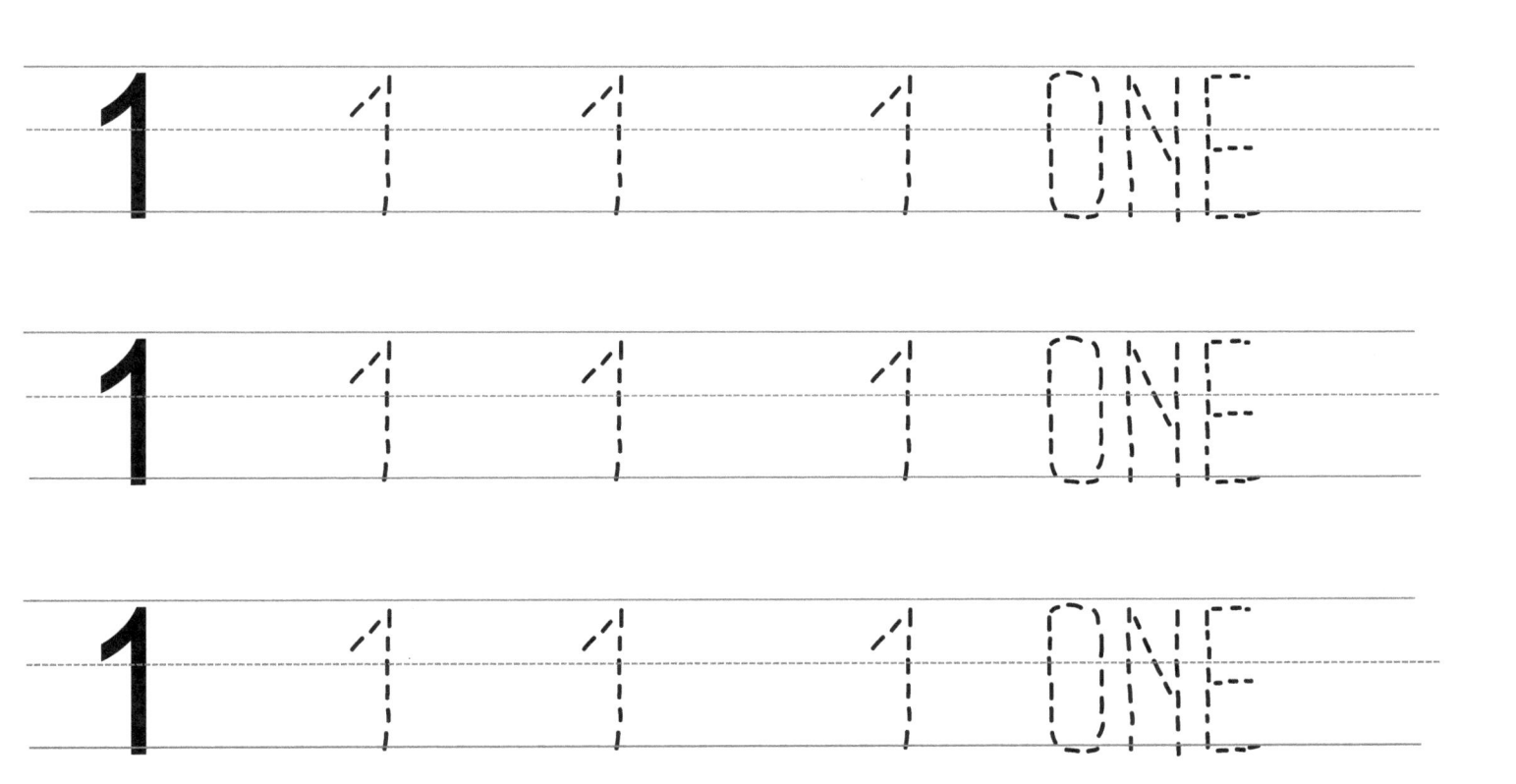

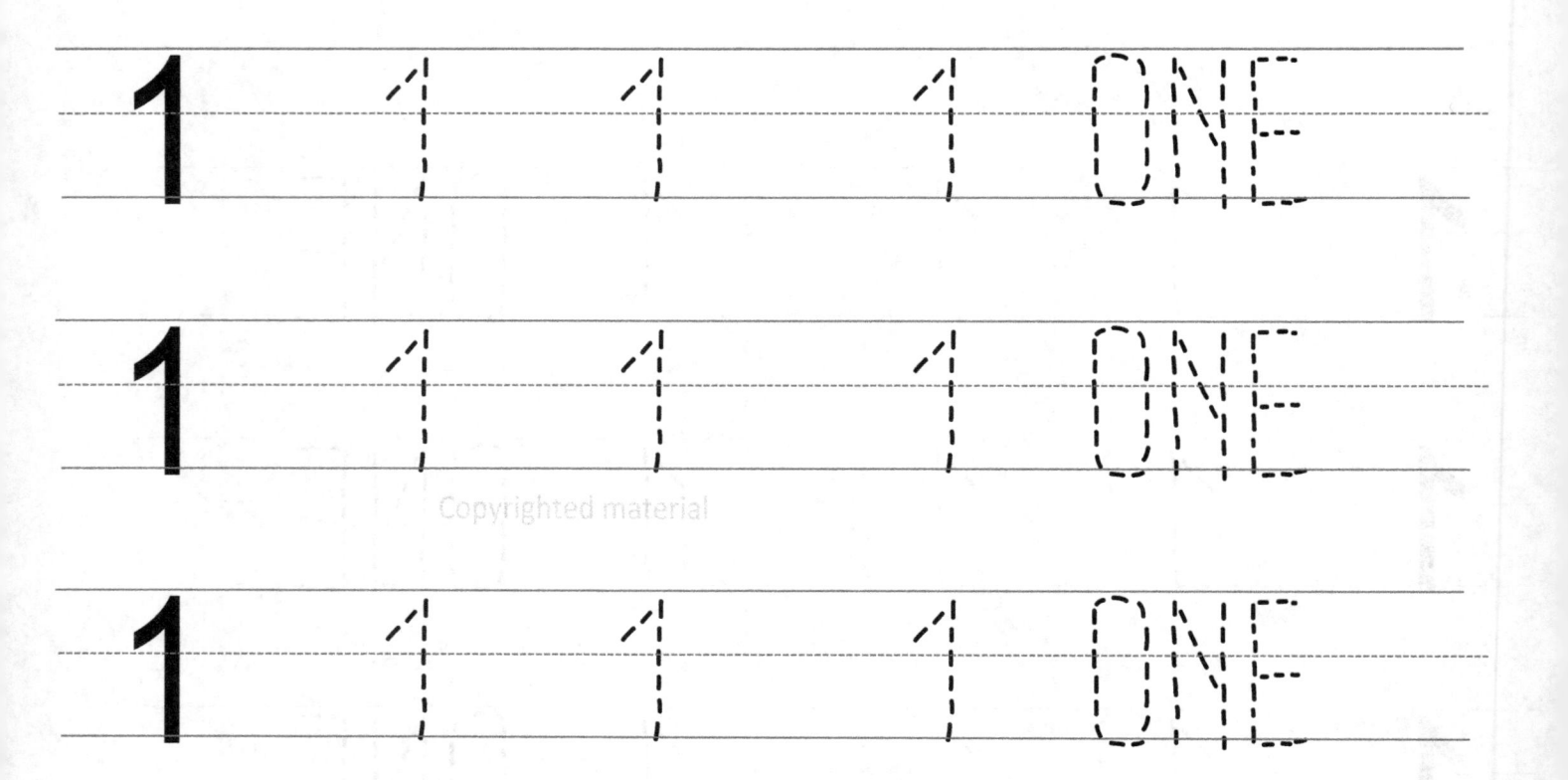

2 2 2 2 TWO

2 2 2 2 TWO

2 2 2 2 TWO

2   2   2   2   TWO

2   2   2   2   TWO

2   2   2   2   TWO

2   2   2   2   TWO

2   2   2   2   TWO

2   2   2   2   TWO

3 3 3 3 THREE

3 3 3 3 THREE

3 3 3 3 THREE

3   3   3   3 THREE

3   3   3   3 THREE

3   3   3   3 THREE

3   3   3   3 THREE

3   3   3   3 THREE

3   3   3   3 THREE

4   4   4   4   FOUR

4   4   4   4   FOUR

4   4   4   4   FOUR

4 4 4 4 FOUR

4 4 4 4 FOUR

4 4 4 4 FOUR

4   4   4   4   FOUR

4   4   4   4   FOUR

4   4   4   4   FOUR

5 5 5 5 FIVE

5 5 5 5 FIVE

5 5 5 5 FIVE

5 5 5 5 FIVE

5 5 5 5 FIVE

5 5 5 5 FIVE

5 5 5 5 FIVE

5 5 5 5 FIVE

5 5 5 5 FIVE

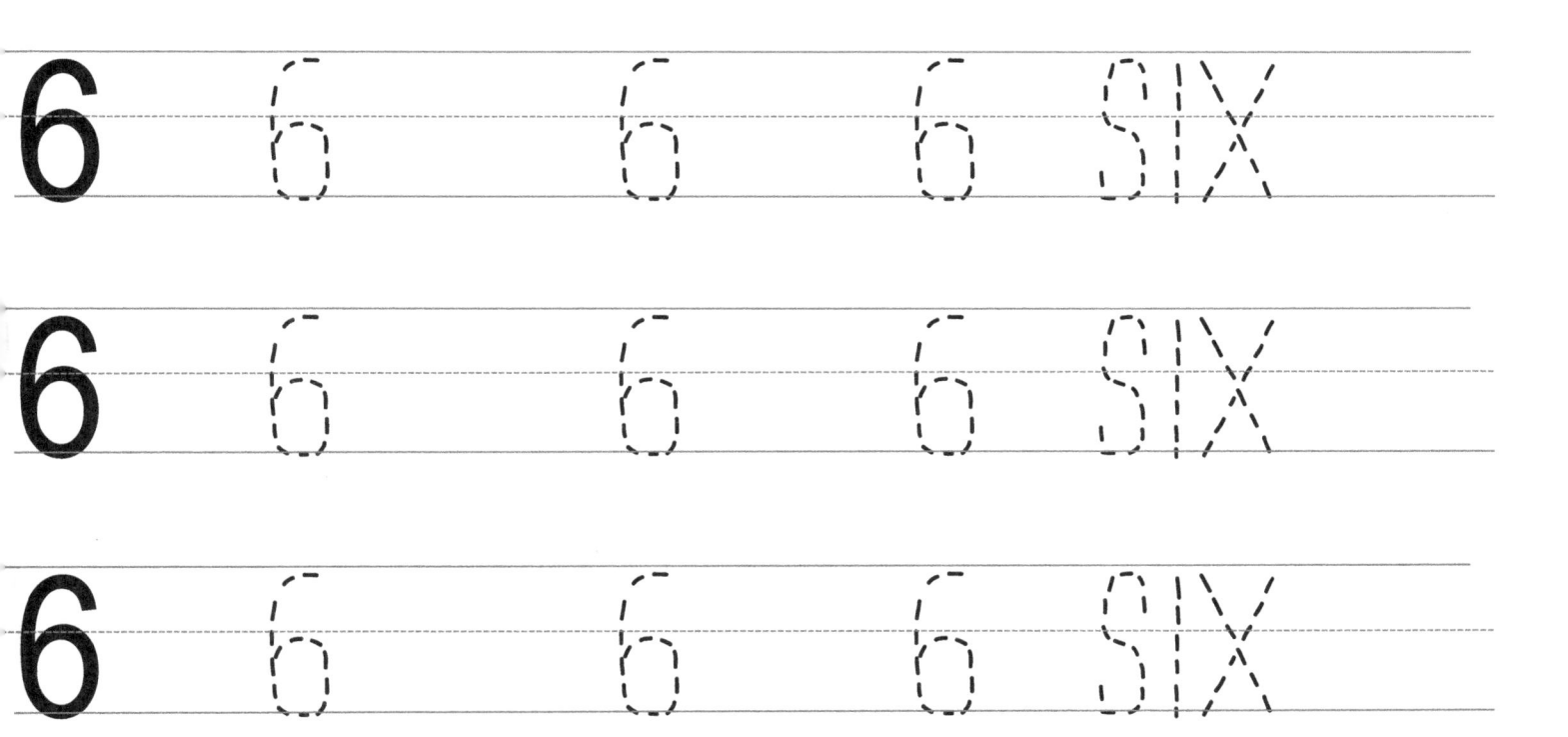

6   6   6   6 SIX

6   6   6   6 SIX

6   6   6   6 SIX

6   6   6   6   SIX

6   6   6   6   SIX

6   6   6   6   SIX

6   6   6   6 SIX

6   6   6   6 SIX

6   6   6   6 SIX

7 7 7 7 SEVEN

7 7 7 7 SEVEN

7 7 7 7 SEVEN

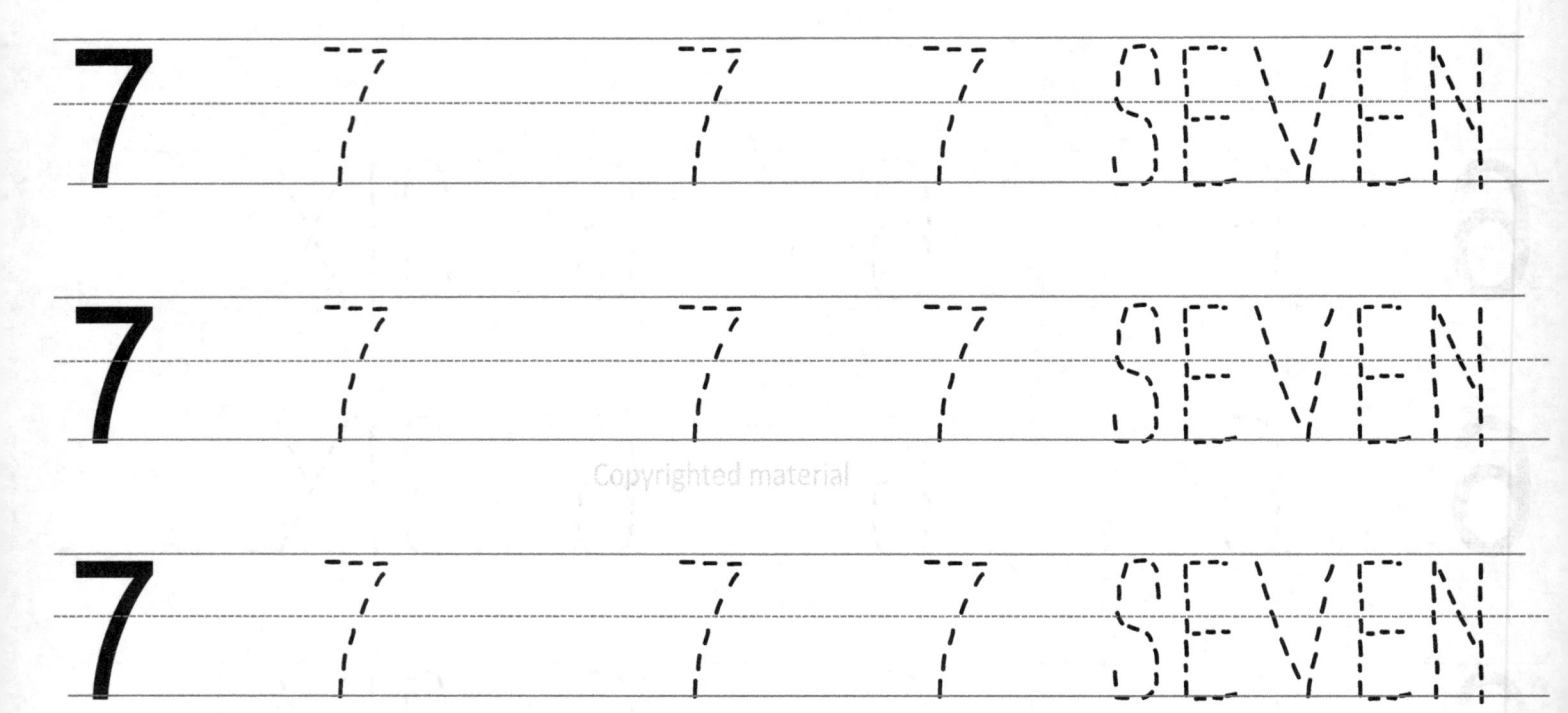

7   7   7   7   SEVEN

7   7   7   7   SEVEN

7   7   7   7   SEVEN

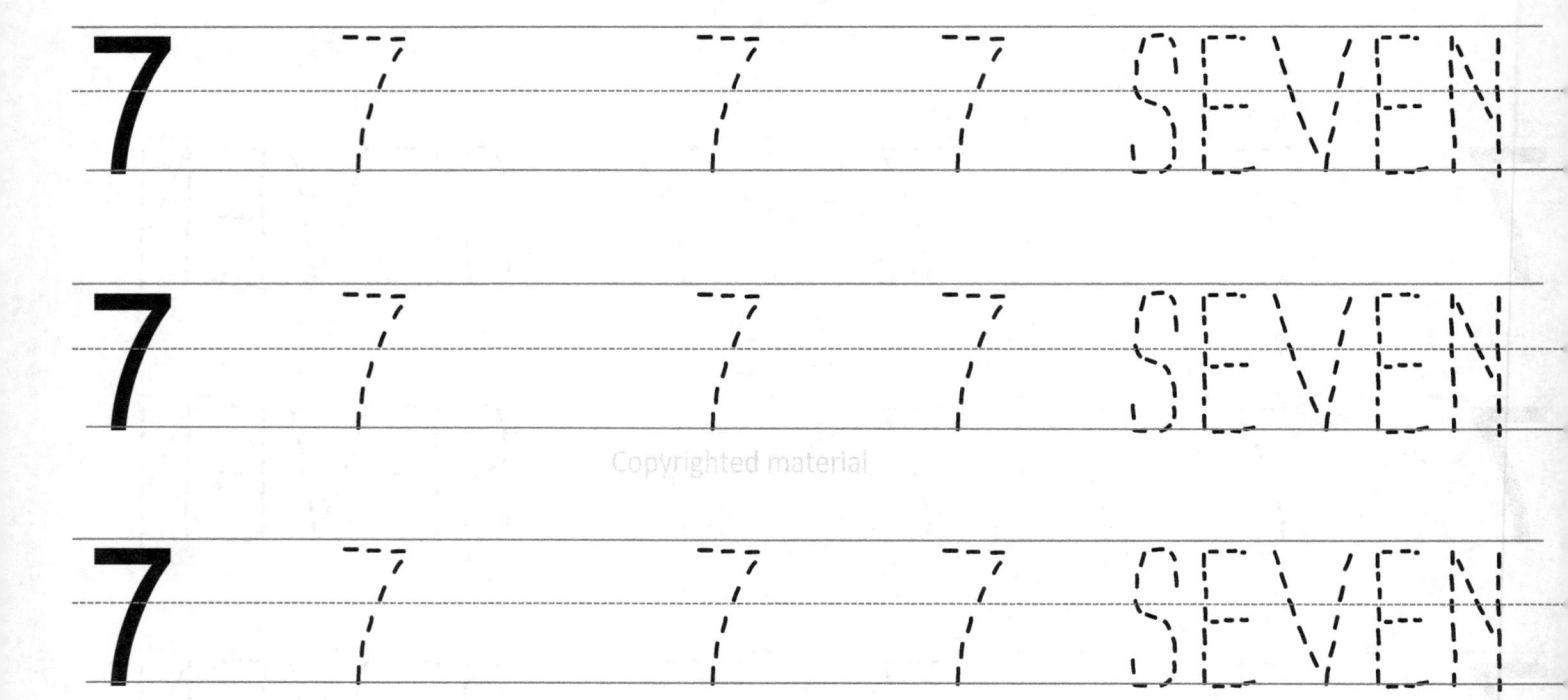

7 7 7 7 SEVEN

7 7 7 7 SEVEN

7 7 7 7 SEVEN

8 8 8 8 EIGHT

8 8 8 8 EIGHT

8 8 8 8 EIGHT

8 8   8   8 EIGHT

8 8   8   8 EIGHT

8 8   8   8 EIGHT

8   8   8   8 EIGHT

8   8   8   8 EIGHT

8   8   8   8 EIGHT

9   9   9   9 NINE

9   9   9   9 NINE

9   9   9   9 NINE

9   9   9   9   9 NINE

9   9   9   9   9 NINE

9   9   9   9   9 NINE

9   9   9   9 NINE

9   9   9   9 NINE

9   9   9   9 NINE

10   10   10   TEN

10   10   10   TEN

10   10   10   TEN

10   10   10   TEN

10   10   10   TEN

10   10   10   TEN

10   10   10   TEN

10   10   10   TEN

10   10   10   TEN

11   11   11 ELEVEN

11   11   11 ELEVEN

11   11   11 ELEVEN

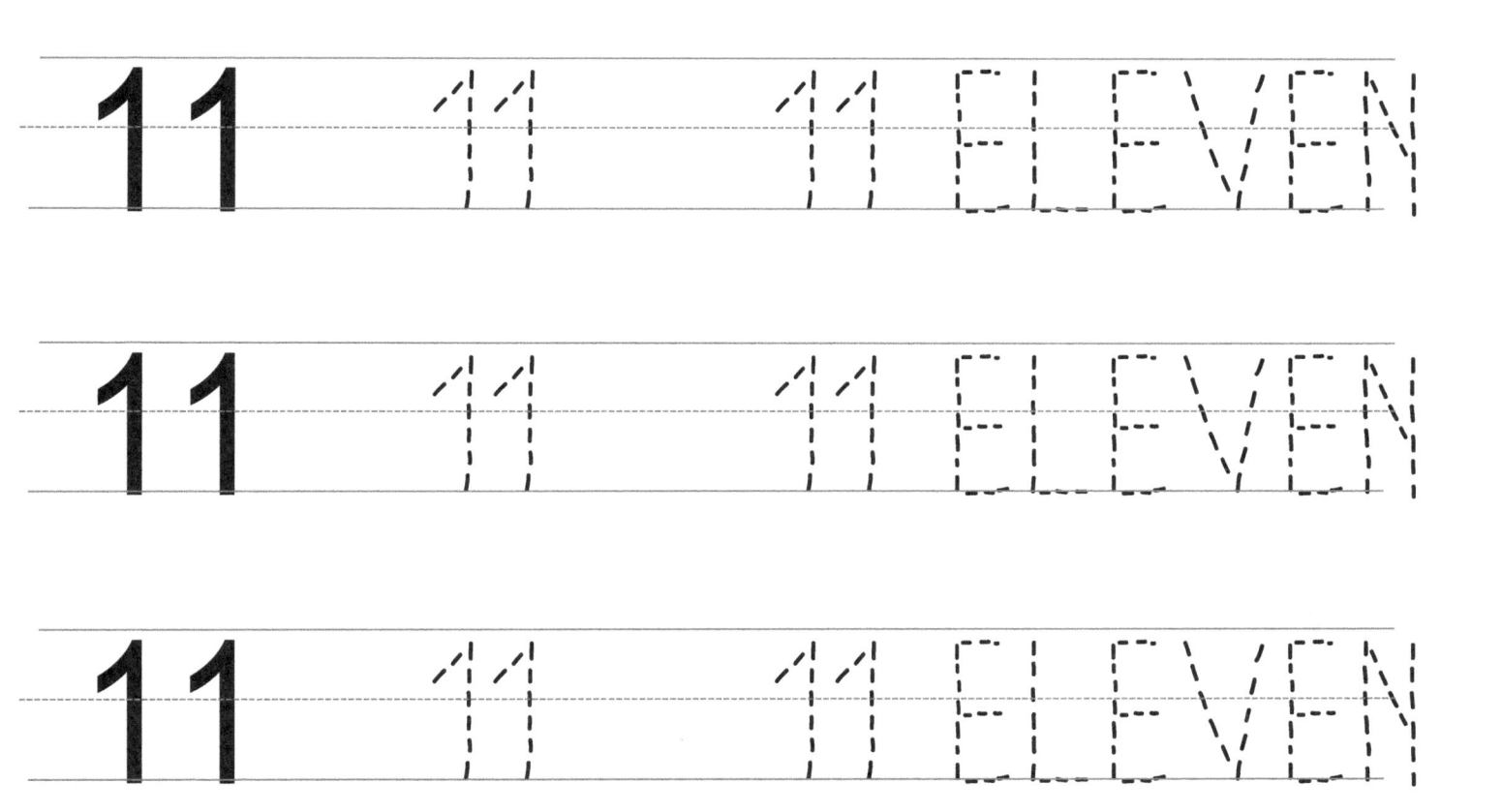

11 11 11 ELEVEN

11 11 11 ELEVEN

11 11 11 ELEVEN

12 12 12 TWELVE

12 12 12 TWELVE

12 12 12 TWELVE

12 12 12 TWELVE

12 12 12 TWELVE

12 12 12 TWELVE

12 12 12 TWELVE

12 12 12 TWELVE

12 12 12 TWELVE

13 13 13 THIRTEEN

13 13 13 THIRTEEN

13 13 13 THIRTEEN

13   13   13   THIRTEEN

13   13   13   THIRTEEN

13   13   13   THIRTEEN

13   13   13 THIRTEEN

13   13   13 THIRTEEN

13   13   13 THIRTEEN

14   14   14   FOURTEEN

14   14   14   FOURTEEN

14   14   14   FOURTEEN

14   14   14   FOURTEEN

14   14   14   FOURTEEN

14   14   14   FOURTEEN

14 14 14 FOURTEEN

14 14 14 FOURTEEN

14 14 14 FOURTEEN

15 15 15 FIFTEEN

15 15 15 FIFTEEN

15 15 15 FIFTEEN

15　15　15　FIFTEEN

15　15　15　FIFTEEN

15　15　15　FIFTEEN

15 15 15 FIFTEEN

15 15 15 FIFTEEN

15 15 15 FIFTEEN

16 16 16 SIXTEEN

16 16 16 SIXTEEN

16 16 16 SIXTEEN

16 16 16 SIXTEEN

16 16 16 SIXTEEN

16 16 16 SIXTEEN

16   16   16   SIXTEEN

16   16   16   SIXTEEN

16   16   16   SIXTEEN

17 17 17 SEVENTEEN

17 17 17 SEVENTEEN

17 17 17 SEVENTEEN

17 17 17 SEVENTEEN

17 17 17 SEVENTEEN

17 17 17 SEVENTEEN

17 17 17 SEVENTEEN

17 17 17 SEVENTEEN

17 17 17 SEVENTEEN

18 18 18 EIGHTEEN

18 18 18 EIGHTEEN

18 18 18 EIGHTEEN

18 18 18 EIGHTEEN

18 18 18 EIGHTEEN

18 18 18 EIGHTEEN

18 18 18 EIGHTEEN

18 18 18 EIGHTEEN

18 18 18 EIGHTEEN

19 19 19 NINETEEN

19 19 19 NINETEEN

19 19 19 NINETEEN

19 19 19 NINETEEN

19 19 19 NINETEEN

19 19 19 NINETEEN

19   19   19   NINETEEN

19   19   19   NINETEEN

19   19   19   NINETEEN

20 20 20 TWENTY

20 20 20 TWENTY

20 20 20 TWENTY

20 20 20 TWENTY

20 20 20 TWENTY

20 20 20 TWENTY

20 20 20 TWENTY

20 20 20 TWENTY

20 20 20 TWENTY

Trace and fill in the dotted numbers.

1   

3   4

5   6

7

8

9

10

Fill in the missing numbers.

1 _____

3 _____

5 _____

8

9